GOD
Why Me?

Kenya Stevenson

Dedications

I dedicate this book to many people for many reasons. Always at the top of my list, Kyla-Jai, Khalil, Dwyer III, Isaac, and Kyurah-Lee, the reasons why I keep going every day and strive to be better than yesterday.

To my best friend, Mario, who was there when I needed someone most and has never stopped being there since the day we met.

To my sister, born from love (not blood), Brande, for always being by my side from the worst days to the best days.

To my brother, born from love (not blood), Robert, who always has a smile, advice, laughs, support, and love for me.

To Reverend Rita M. Henderson, for encouraging and pushing me to find my calling. Most of all, I dedicate this book to Deanna.

One night, one conversation, two women changed forever. The night God spoke through me, the night I felt his love, the night my question was finally answered, the night I finally understood – "God, Why Me?"

Contents

Psalm 23

1. The Lord is my shepherd; I shall not want.

2. He maketh me to lie down in green pastures: he leadeth me beside the still waters.

3. He restoreth my soul: he leadeth me in the paths of righteousness for his name's sake.

4. Yea, though I walk through the valley of the shadow of death, I will fear no evil: for thou art with me; thy rod and thy staff they comfort me.

5. Thou preparest a table before me in the presence of mine enemies: thou anointest my head with oil; my cup runneth over.

6. Surely goodness and mercy shall follow me all the days of my life: and I will dwell in the house of the Lord forever.

Introduction

Locked in a dark room with blades and sharp objects made to impale jutting from every surface, above, below, and all around. Every turn, every bend, any and every movement causes pain. Desperate to escape but too weak to try, you give in and learn to live with the restriction. This is my description of grief. This is the hell that I was locked in and could not escape. The door clearly in my vision and unencumbered; all I have to do is approach the door, reach out my hand to it.

Just as I gain enough strength to raise my arm, the sorrow takes control and reminds me that I am too empty. I was so weak in mind, spirit, and body that I was sure I would not survive this pain and devastation. Walking around the earth completely detached, lost. Days and weeks pass by, but the pain remains the same, and now I am quite sure this room of torture and punishment that I have managed to close myself into is getting smaller. As the walls begin to close in, I become anxious and nervous, wondering why I'm the only one locked into such a desolate place.

Everything in my life began to fall apart in 1998 when I lost my beloved granny to lung cancer. I knew she was sick and had decided to choose quality of life over quantity of life, so somehow her death was a relief for me. My granny suffered tremendously during the end, so when God finally called her home, I was happy for her. This was my first real experience with grief. I was sad and sorry that my beloved grandmother would no longer be there. I was already missing the Sunday dinners and visits. To see my grandmother finally be free and out of pain was worth way more than any visit with her for me. My mother did not find the same solace. My mother was destroyed by her mother's passing. She never recovered from her grief, and ultimately that coupled with bipolarism, led to her suicide three years later.

Losing my mother to suicide changed my life forever and left me scared so deep that the wounds still remain to this day. Six years later, my sweet baby son died in his sleep due to SIDS. This pain reduced me to a puddle on the floor, my heart liquified, my soul dissolved. Were it not for the love of my dear husband and God; I would not be here to tell this story.

Yet, nine short years later, my soul mate died on the kitchen floor of a massive heart attack at the age of 35. In between these deaths, I lost countless family members, including my stepfather, my father in law, and my aunt, who was a family matriarch. The funerals became like weekly family reunions that have left me at this point today, unable to attend funerals anymore.

With each and every death, I found myself at odds with God. Each and every time, God would come to me and make me strong, uplift me, hold me, comfort me, love me. Each time I found myself not quite the same, broken, somehow. I always had the same question, "Why me?"

I know now that all the pain and loss that I have endured was not in vain, and more importantly, it was not a punishment. It was for me to be in this position right now to share my story and help others that may be feeling trapped by grief and lost as to how to move on with their life. For so long, I was trapped, hurting, and had so many questions that I wanted answers to. I would partially heal from one death, just to be hit by another and another. I was overwhelmed and depressed and could not find my way out. I looked and looked for some type of help. I was not in a dark place; I was just so hurt and confused. I would try to talk to people, but they would all tell me that what I was feeling was normal. All I could think was, what about this was normal?

I read numerous books that spoke of the steps of grief and how I just had to give it time and go through the steps. Except, none of the clinical steps to grief applied to me. There are five stages to grief; 1. Denial, 2. Anger, 3. Bargaining, 4. Depression, 5. Acceptance. I never had any denial, I knew exactly what was happening, and I was fully aware there was no changing it. I was definitely angry, very angry, but there was no bargaining with God; I wanted answers. Whether I was ready or not, acceptance was inevitable. Depression was the thing that I was not prepared for. With each death, it was different, so much that different, that I had no idea I was even depressed sometimes.

With all that being said, I hope to give you all the information I have now, about all the things I had to find out the hard way. So that people can have some type of understanding from my view of things. I would not consider myself an expert on the subject, but I definitely have quite a lot of experience.

As a child, we are taught to believe. To believe in something larger than ourselves. As Christians, we are taught about God. Our wonderful God that created the heavens and the earth in six days and on the seventh day he rested. We are taught that we are all the children of God, and as his children, we will always be loved and cared for by him.

With believing comes faith. Having faith can be a tricky course to navigate. Having faith should be easy, right? When things are good in life, it is so easy for us to thank God. Also, when we wake up in the morning and thank God for another day. When unexpected money comes our way, we praise God, "God is good, all the time!!" We go to church to be reminded of God's love, to praise his name, to hear, and learn his word. For some people, faith is simple; it's a deep-rooted movement, embedded. Whether things are good or bad, we talk to God.

For some people, faith is just not that easy. For some faith is just a novelty. Believing in God and having faith that he will always be there, although you can't see or touch him. When you were born into and live in a world of tangibles, this can be a difficult obstacle. People tend to only believe in what they can hold in hand or see with their own eyes. In our world right now, even hope has almost become extinct. People who are educated and rooted in science sometimes find it almost impossible to believe in something larger than themselves. This is where strong faith comes into play, to be able to praise God when things are at their worst.

To go through things and know you will come out the other end, smarter, stronger, and enlightened because you know that God walks with you. To know, really know, with every ounce in your being that no matter what, God will work it out. That is faith at its finest, God is good, all day, every day. Are those just words to you? Or do you really believe it?

I ask this question of you because faith is everything when dealing with grief.

Believe in God's Words

> *"God is not a man, that he should lie, neither the son of man, that he should repent: Hath he said, and will he not do it? Or hath he spoken, and will he not make it good?"*

> *(Numbers 23:19)*

Death sucks in every way, and there is no changing that. I never really knew that until one hot, summer day in July, July 18, 2001, to be exact. I was trying to call my mother on the phone. This was before cellular phones became a permanent fixture on every person's hands. It was so hot out that day; the sweat was beading on my forehead before I had a chance to wave my fan for a small bit of relief. I was getting no answer from my mother's house where I was calling. I was beginning to become concerned and anxious. I received a call from her late the night before; I knew something was wrong, and I really needed to hear her voice. I needed to know she was alright.

The phone rang again, with no answer. At that point, I jumped in the car and set off on the twenty-minute drive to her house, dreading what I may find. I fought with my mind the whole way to avoid all the horrible things that were brewing. I turned on her tree-lined street, and as I approached her house, I could see her car in the driveway that confirmed that she was indeed at home. I pulled in the front of her pristine yellow house with all the beautiful flowers on the porch. Every step had its own perfect pot that contained a unique and special flower that always seemed happy to me in some way. Plants hung from the roof swaying in the wind with skinny green tendrils that drip pretty pink petals. Two lovely little chairs were on the porch for conversations with neighbours about how green and thick her lawn was.

I knocked on the door and waited for her to answer. I knocked again and waited, soon the knocks became bangs. After what seemed like forever, I began to bang on the door frantically with both hands and screaming out, "Mom? It's me, are you there?" Nothing but silence would be my answer. My worst fears were quickly becoming a reality, and I was not prepared for what lay ahead. I knew I had to get into her house, so an open window in her bedroom would have to serve as my makeshift entrance. I climbed to the window and broke through the screen as I toppled to the bedroom floor. My first thought is to find my mother as I stand to my feet. I turned to walk out of her room when I got that feeling, the feeling that makes all the hairs on your neck stand up. I slowly turned my head; there she was, dead in her bed. Her blonde hair was stringy from the heat and wrapped over her face. I broke out in a cold sweat, I was in shock, the whole room looked foggy, and I was moving in slow motion. The woman in me kicked in, and I was able to call the authorities, handle all the calls to the family with the bad news. I just went into autopilot, moving about handling business, never fazed by what had just really happened.

On the night of my mother's funeral, I broke down. I had held it all together, stayed strong. I was the pillar of strength with a mask that could not be penetrated. I had to be there for my young kids who did not understand death at all, let alone why Nanna had to die. I was the only child; I had a funeral to plan. I had to get all her affairs in order. There was no time for grief, no time for tears.

That night, after all the hugs had been given, and all the condolences had been said. Once all the people had gone, and the silence fell upon the house. Then the true pain of what had really happened here began to set in; I really began to realize that I was going to have to face life without my best friend. My one true shield against all the hurt, my safe place, my mommy was gone. The pain hit my chest like someone swung a baseball bat and hit me full force. I was lost, angry, confused, and I flat out blamed God for all her pain and hurt. All I could say was, "God, why me?" I heard no answer. I was convinced. I was alone. My faith was weak. I was weak. At that moment, the wall broke, and all the emotions started to flow. I screamed out for my mom; I called to her, feeling like there was no way I was going to make it. I fell on my knees and asked God to please take this pain from me. I told God, it hurt to take a breath. There on the floor, I pleaded with God, "If you expect me to carry on and be a mother and a wife after this blow, then I needed some help." I begged with tears flowing so hard that a puddle was forming at my knees.

Right there on that floor in my bathroom, something in my head said just breathe. I took a deep breath and exhaled, with that breath, my heart was saddened but no longer broken.

Through all the pain and tears, I sat on that bathroom floor with a smile on my face, a warmth in my heart. Nothing in this world can compare to the feeling of love and comfort that flowed through me. Not even the warmth of my mother's arms could compare to this feeling.

Psalm 145:18 says,

"The Lord is near to all who call upon him, to all who call upon him in truth."

At that moment, I was restored. I tell you my story so that you may know the power of our God when you are in your time of need. I stood in direct defiance of God. I cursed his name and questioned his power. Yet still, when I fell to my knees and called his name, he was there. I began to read the book of Psalms, and it gave me strength. The words of God reassured me that as long as I did not forsake him, he would not forsake me. From that point on, I knew he was there. My faith was strong; my relationship with God renewed.

I faced the next days and months with my bible and God's love as my shield. I had many days that I felt like it just was not enough. On those days, I never had to rely on faith alone because he was always there. The strength would come from nowhere, the voice in my head that says, "Yes, you can."

"The Lord himself goes before you and will be with you; he will never leave you nor forsake you. Do not be afraid; do not be discouraged"

(Deuteronomy 31:8).

The words of God are a forever comfort if you only take the time to look for it.

Anger is Okay, Don't Be Absorbed by It

"Be angry and yet do not sin; Do not let the sun go down on your anger"

(Ephesians 4:26).

Anger walks side by side with grief. One could even say that they are the same. How can someone experience the loss of a loved one and not be angry about it? It's a natural human response to loss or hurt. The problem with grief is it's so very easy for us to become lost in our own anger and pain. We hurt so badly when death occurs that we want to hurt those that cause us this pain. But who caused this pain? Was it God? Was it you? Was it them?

Six long years had slowly tipped by since my mother passed away; with a lot of prayer and love from friends and family, I was able to overcome her tragic and sudden loss. With much scripture and study, my relationship with God had become whole again. Life had returned to a new normal, and I was coping. At this point, a lot had changed for my family and me since the death of my mother. I had my first real taste of depression, and I was struggling to hold life together. Keeping a job was proving to be very difficult for me at this time. My mental state made it very hard to stay organized. My children suffered during this time, as I kept forgetting school projects and appointments. My husband was extremely affected by the events and ultimately was no support for me.

I drowned my pain and sorrows in money. I shopped and spent to keep from feeling empty. This was depression, but I had no idea. I spent myself into debt, and by the time I realized it was too late. My marriage came to an end but not before we had two more children. I was finding it hard to keep my faith again due to all the pain I was experiencing. I could not understand what I had done to deserve all this hardship in my life. I was just getting my life back on track; I had a new relationship and on a happy path for a new life. The kids were happy and adjusting to our new life and our new family when disaster struck.

It was a cold morning in January 2007, the first day back to school after Christmas break.

We were getting ready to walk to school, and I sent my daughter (the oldest) upstairs to get the sleeping baby from his bed. I wanted to move him to the bed with my husband in case he woke while I was walking the kids to school. While my daughter was upstairs, I slipped into my bedroom to slide on some layers for the snowy walk. I heard a knock at the door, knowing it was my daughter with the baby, I called for her to open the door and come in. The door never opened; I called out again, "come in." At the door, all I heard is this small voice say, "I think there is something wrong with the baby, he is very cold, and he is not moving." My husband jumped from the bed, grabbed the doorknob, and snatched the door open.

There in the doorway stood my sweet ten-year-old daughter holding her dead brother. My chubby little fat baby was cold, stiff, frozen in the angelic position he was sleeping in when he slipped away in the night. Mom mode kicked in, and I tried frantically to give him CPR. I tried to bring him back, whispering prayers under my breath as I pumped on his little chest. My husband called 911 while he watched me try everything I knew to try to bring life back into this baby. Soon the EMS arrived, and they grabbed up my baby boy and sprinted to the ambulance. They put me in the front seat, and with lights flashing and sirens blaring, we rushed to the children's hospital.

As soon as we pulled in, doctors came, and before I could blink an eye, the stretcher with my son on it was gone. I stood there looking at the empty ambulance, frozen, unable to move. A nurse grabbed my hand and led me to a row of chairs in a long white hallway. It was hollow, scary, not another person in sight. I sat in the chair, shaking, tearing up a piece of a napkin the nurse had given me to wipe my face. All I could do was sit and whisper sad pleas to God, please God, not my baby, please God not again.

After what seemed like an eternity, a doctor appears and looks at me. Before she could even fix her lips to speak, I already knew what she was there to say. "I am so sorry, but we have done all that we could, your baby didn't survive." Those words would set my life on a path of destruction for the next almost two years. Again I found myself wrapped in depression. This time I found myself making awful decisions all around. I was in a deep hole where I just did not care. I wanted to be numb from the pain. I didn't want to think of my loss. Living without my child was more than I could carry at the time. I lost myself in drugs and parties. I would disappear from reality for days frolicking in a drug-induced fantasy land where I did not have responsibilities.

Alcohol replaced my morning coffee, and my days would melt into nights with no end. My children were lost in the wind going from my ex-husband to me and back again with zero stability in between. The death of my baby boy left me flat out mad! No, this time, there was no scripture to make this all better. This pain was unbelievable, one that I would not wish on my worst enemy. No mother, ever, deserves to feel the pain of holding her dead child, no matter the age. This time I was furious, and I had a beef with God. My baby!!! My baby? There was no way anyone was going to make me make sense of this one. I walked around with that anger in me for the next year or more. That anger made me go to drugs for comfort instead of God, and also made me look for comfort in people who were not my friends. That anger made me question the love my father had for me, made me ignore my love for my living children. There were not enough tears to extinguish this inferno burning in my soul, or so I thought.

I was closed off to God in every way, in my heart, my mind, and my soul. No church, no reading, no studying, nothing. He was not there, and if he was, he definitely did not love me. I had convinced myself that there was no way to heal from a loss like this. My God found a way to speak to me to soften my heart once again. He sent me a daughter to love, to remind me of his love, and to assure me that life will go on through the pain. That little life inside me gave me the strength to come back from the darkness into the light of God again.

I began to pray to God for the strength to walk away from the drugs. I slowly came back to myself and began to put the pieces of my life back together. Day by day, prayer by prayer, I got stronger. My children came home again, where they began to flourish and grow again. We began going to church again, and our lives were improving on all levels. I never got the answer to my question, but I was on a path to healing with my God by my side.

No one said that life was easy; no one said that there would be no pain or suffering. God never said, "Believe in me, and you will never suffer again." There is no scripture to read that will tell you that a life with God means no death, no hunger, and no pain.

John 16:33 tells us,

"I have told you of these things, so that in me you may have peace. In this world, you will have trouble. But take heart, I have overcome the world."

What God is telling us is, the world will bring the pain and troubles, but he is the remedy. God does not take people from us to punish us or make us learn lessons. Death is a part of life that we must all bear and deal with at some point in our lives. God gives us lessons to be learned in our losses and hard times so that we may appreciate what we have and not take the simple things for granted.

We can always ask God for understanding and help with our anger. Knowing that you are stronger than your feelings is what God needs us to know. He won't change your feelings; what he will change is you. He will make you stronger, even stronger than the anger inside you.

Sometimes You Have to Make Your Own Closure

"In all your ways acknowledge him, and he shall direct your paths."

(Proverbs 3:6).

When death and loss occur, sometimes you get lucky. I use the word lucky because when a loved one is terminally ill, you are halfway prepared for the outcome, positive or negative, whatever that may be. Like in the situation with my sweet granny, I knew what was coming, so I had time to make sense of it. I knew the who, what, when, where, and most importantly, the why.

These situations are a little bit easier to deal with because you have closure. You knew what was coming and had the time to make arrangements, resolve old issues, say your goodbyes and be ready for what may come. Not all of us have that luxury. For a lot of people, death comes as a total surprise. We get that random phone call from a relative to break the bad news. Sadly, sometimes your story goes like mine.

My mother died of suicide. I had no say, no time to say goodbye. I was left with nothing but questions, with no answers to be found. Completely consumed with pain and torment, I decided to take on this self-appointed quest to get the answers only my mother had. I spent hours researching suicide online. I was reading a heart-breaking story after heart-breaking story, hoping to find just one thing to make me understand why she had done this.

The more I looked, the more questions I had. This behaviour became my prison. The answers to the questions would be my key to earn my release from this jail. The days that made up my sentence would come and go, and each day would prove to be a failure—no more answers than I had the day before.

One night with nothing but the glow of the computer monitor to illuminate the room, I became still sitting at my desk. With my elbows on the desk, I rested my face in my hands, rubbing my forehead with my fingertips. I was distraught, sitting staring at the bright screen, wondering where to look next for these answers I so desperately sought. I had to find the answer.

I had to know why my mother would choose to end her own life. Mostly I think I wanted to know what I had done wrong. I was sure that I had messed up, dropped the ball somehow. I sat there thinking when the tears began to drop upon the wood surface. In my head, I heard a voice clear as a bell, "The answer is not somewhere to be found." This was not the voice of a stranger but rather the voice of my mother. I spoke out into the darkness, asking, "Then where?"

Sitting right there on the corner of the desk where it always sat was the bible. I reached straight for the book, opened it, and began to read. No particular book or verse just opened it up. Although I had not made peace with her death, I slowly found myself feeling like the answers were not so important anymore. The more I prayed, the less it mattered.

That is until June 20, 2015, when my dear husband had a massive heart attack on the kitchen floor after returning from a family fishing trip. Again, tons of questions, no one to answer them. I found myself calling all of his doctors looking for someone to blame, some procedure that was missed, and some mistake that was made. There was none to be found, no doctor to blame. With both deaths, I found myself mentally and emotionally drained. Every speck of thought I had was on them, and all my unanswered questions. Again, I was caught in a tailspin that I could not break free from.

What I didn't know then was, what I was looking for in both cases was closure. I needed a reason, something for my brain to wrap around for it to make sense to me. I wanted to know why this was happening. It's another one of those human responses to grief; we all cope in different ways.

For me, my hair was falling out; my weight had dropped, my eyes were heavy with deep circles. As I kept trying to find answers, I was sent a message. I don't really remember how or where it came to me, but the scripture,

Proverbs 3:5-6

"Trust in the Lord with all your heart and lean not on your own understanding; in all your ways submit to him, and he will make your path straight."

With that message, once again, I was whole again. Armoured once again with the words of God against my own feelings. Once again, he swept in and saved me. Once again, he was there to relieve my pain and twisted thoughts. Once again, my faith had led me to the answers I sought.

The answer was simple all along; "Give it to God." Put all your worries and anxiety in his hands, and he will worry for you. He will carry the burden; it is simply not my battle. It was never meant for me to understand; what was meant for me is to trust in God that he has given me all the information I needed.

The closure I was seeking was in the hands of God. All I needed to do was ask. Now, by no means am I saying that I just don't think of it anymore. My mind is strong, and my heart can be weak. I find myself thinking and wondering some days, but for my own health and well being I must remind myself there will be a bunch of things that I will never know when it comes to figuring out a plan that was never mine to understand.

Forgiving and Forgiveness is required for Self Love

"Forbearing one another, and forgiving one another, if any man has a quarrel against any; even as Christ forgave you, so do also ye"

(Colossians 3:13).

I want to talk about forgiveness because, for so many, when we are in pain, we tend to take the blame upon ourselves. We tend to believe had we done something different; the outcome would have been different in some way. We tend to tell ourselves had we been a better child, wife, husband, sister, brother, friend; the situation would somehow be different. The truth of the matter is most of the time that is just not true.

I found every reason in the book that if I had just been a better daughter, my mother would never have killed herself. I would sit and think to myself of dinners that I cancelled on or birthdays I forgot. The heaviest to carry was the phone call I received hours before she killed herself.

It was a Saturday night at around ten o'clock. The kids were in bed, and I had just put my seven-day-old baby to bed. I was so ready to have just a few minutes of peace when the phone rang. It was my mother, in another spiral. My mother battled with bipolarism for most of her life. She constantly battled with her illness and her medications. The medications made her feel like a zombie, so she often decided to stop taking them, causing her emotions to spiral out of control. When this happens, she would often call crying, manically depressed.

15

For me, this became an exhausting dance of consoling her, reasoning with her, convincing her to take her meds again. She would agree, all would be right again until it wasn't again. That night I just did not have the energy to deal with it. She wanted to talk to my daughter, who was in bed, sleeping. I said, "No," which caused her to cry uncontrollably.

I eventually took the phone to my daughter, who tried to talk through her sleepy haze and let them have their phone time. When she was done talking to my daughter, she tried to talk to me, but I rushed her off the phone because I just could not listen to her anymore that day. I promised to call her in the morning, and all she kept saying was how much she loved my kids and me. I reassured her that I knew how much she loved us and that we would talk first thing in the morning. Unknown to me that would be the last time I would ever speak to my mother.

After the funeral and all that came with it and I tried to carry on with life. I was racked with guilt. I felt very responsible for my mother's suffering. I found myself trying to make up for it in different ways within my life. I would overly buy things for my children. Giving them any and everything they wanted in hopes that I would not disappoint anyone else. I truly believed it was all my fault. I should have stayed on the phone with her longer; I should have made more of an effort; the list of reasons I had was endless.

I knew that my mother suffered from bipolarism, but for me, that was a non-factor. It was my fault, and I was prepared to carry that for the rest of my life. I would carry that guilt, pain, embarrassment, and humiliation in my mind, my stomach, my back, and, most of all, in my heart for the next almost twenty years. I only just recently was able to let that part go when I had to deal with the guilt all over again when I lost my husband.

My husband went into renal failure at the age of 27. We found out about his health issues when he complained that it was getting hard to work on cars because his vision was blurry.

One day he got a really bad headache, bad enough that he wanted to go to the hospital to be examined. When he was being checked into the emergency department, the nurses checked his temperature and blood pressure. That's when we found out his blood pressure was so high he was in the danger zone for a stroke.

The only issue was he felt fine, except for a headache. In the next twelve hours in that hospital, we were told that his blurry vision was due to the high blood pressure. Not only would his vision not be returning, but it would progressively get worse, leaving him legally blind in the end. Also, due to the blood pressure, his kidneys were failing, and it could not be reversed. In the next two weeks, my husband would end up on dialysis, and stay there for the next seven years waiting for a kidney transplant.

On June 22, 2013, we got the call that they had a kidney for him. He went off to surgery, and we were all so relieved that this nightmare was soon to be over. No more dialysis three times a week. No more sitting in chairs with needles and tubes for hours. He could finally eat and drink whatever he wanted again. He came out of surgery, and he was on the healing train.

In the next years, life was so good for us; I went back to work; he was living life again. Two years later, on June 20, 2015, my husband was walking in the door from a family fishing trip, and he fell to the floor. He was not breathing, but his heart was beating. I had my aunt call 911 while I started CPR. My husband lay there on the hard floor with grown men pounding on his chest.

I, along with two of our sons and our five-year-old daughter, stood there helpless and watched as the paramedics tried to save his life. His heart would beat, then stop, beat, then stop, all the while the paramedics are trying to get him to the hospital. I followed behind the ambulance in a police car, watching EMS struggle to stay on the road. They were still pounding on his chest the whole way.

By the time we reached the hospital, my sweet husband had given up. They wheeled his body into the room and hooked up the monitors, but there was nothing there. Just straight lines and that horrible solid tone of death that rings in alarm. He was gone, and I was left there alone.

In the weeks preceding his funeral, I was in touch with all of his doctors. I was astounded as to how my husband was dead. He has just gotten his new kidney that was supposed to solve all our problems. He was well, what happened? This is when I found out that the new kidney had failed.

The doctors told my husband that he needed to return to dialysis immediately and that he would be placed back on the transplant list. My husband was supposed to go to dialysis on the day we left for the fishing trip. He never told me, never told me he was sick, never said the kidney had failed. My love knew exactly what would happen if he didn't get dialysis. He knew that trip would be his last; he also knew he would not make it home.

His doctors explained to me that they had a long talk with my husband, and he was fully aware that his situation was dire. At that point, I had to realize that he made a clear choice to give up. Then my mind began to spin; the questions started to form. Then all the guilt came rolling in like thunder.

My biggest issue is, why couldn't he talk to me? I was so hurt that he didn't tell me, I couldn't figure out what I had done to make him feel like he couldn't share this with me. Then I began to manifest all the fear he must have had in those last days. How it must have felt to walk around on vacation with his smiling kids, knowing his time with us was so limited. I was flooded with heartbreak and drowning in my own emotions and guilt.

This time, the death, the guilt took me to an ugly, dark place. I was wrapped tight in depression. I was detached and sad. I wanted out this time; I wanted to go. I decided I no longer had the strength to deal with this pain.

I was speaking with a co-worker at the time, who would later become my best friend. I called him, desperate for a friend to talk to so that I would not hurt myself. I explained that I just needed a friend. He asked if he could come by and see me. Not long later, his vehicle pulled along the curb outside my home. I was relieved to have someone near to pull me back from the edge.

He could see the pain in me from a mile away, and he asked, "You need to talk?" I sat there with him and cried; I spoke of all my pain and told him how I was giving up on my life. He grabbed my shoulders and said to me, "Whatever it is, let it go, you have to forgive her and him."

Those words at that moment were all that I needed to bring me back to reality. My friend went on to tell me how it was okay for me to be sad. How I needed to let all my pain flow, but that God was always there for me. He filled me up with the word of God through song, love, and laughter. I was so hurt, so sad that it never occurred to me that I needed to forgive her and him for leaving me behind, for leaving me and not being honest, not saying goodbye.

Most of all, I needed to forgive myself. I needed to heal from the destruction I had brought upon myself. I had decided in my mind that this was my cross to bear. When in reality, it fell on God to carry that burden, I needed only to hand it to him. I learned to let it go, I learned to pray for forgiveness for my lost loved ones, and I learned not only to ask for God to forgive me but for the strength and understanding to forgive myself.

"Do not judge and you will not be judged. Do not condemn, and you will not be condemned. Forgive, and you will be forgiven" *(Luke 6:37).*

We must let go of the hurt and give the same compassion to our lost loved ones that God gave to us. If you want to be blessed, you must forgive. Most importantly, when dealing with grief, forgiveness is for yourself. So that you may be strong enough to endure. Guilt will tear you apart from the inside out. It will affect you physically, mentally, and emotionally until you have nothing left, and it destroys you.

You Have So Much to Live For

"Though your beginning was small, yet your latter end should greatly increase"

(Job 8:7).

A huge lesson I had to learn is remembering the living and my faith. I had to remember that I was important and that this pain and this wound would get better with time. We are so consumed with pain and the loss that we forget to live; we forget that God has provided this wonderful place for us to be a part of. We slide off into depression and don't know how to live for ourselves. It's almost like we forget how.

Dark rooms with glowing televisions become the new night club. Meals are eaten in bed; showers become less and less important. We forget that we are still alive and have so much to live for. I was hit with depression the worst with the death of my husband. I drew away and hid under the covers. I tried my best to handle the daily tasks that come with being a mom. Most days, I was a complete failure. I was sad every day, all day, all I could do was cry till my eyes burned.

People die every day, but when it hits us personally, we tend to feel like no one else can understand what we are feeling or going through. I thank God for my family and friends in my circle that never let me drift too far away. Depression is real and can take hold of you without you even realizing it. I found myself in a very dark place that made me have thoughts of not being around anymore.

God knows I was so very close to taking that final step. That's why he sent me a friend in my time of need to talk me off the ledge and back to the love that was surrounding me. Lots of people suffer from different levels of depression. It can range from mild to manic, with symptoms ranging from simple sadness to self-harm. I never even saw the difference until I found myself at the lowest point. If you feel like you may want to harm yourself in any way, I implore you to talk to someone and tell them how you are feeling.

What most don't see is we can get ahead of the depression before it even tries to set in.

Staying active and eating is essential for beating the blues. Although we may not be ready to jump back into regular life, we must get out of the house. We have to stay active, take a walk, ride a bike, sit at the park and watch the birds, anything to keep you from sinking into an ocean of sadness that will eventually overtake you.

Before my husband died, I would walk miles every day. It was my release, and my time to clear my mind. I had to find a reason to go on every day, so my walks became a daily commitment, one daily goal to reach and feel rewarded. Soon I was back to putting in miles and feeling emotionally stronger with each and every step.

Eating is probably the most difficult to deal with during a time of loss. When we feel low, the first thing to leave us is our appetite. Eating is the last thing on your mind, and just about everything seems unappetizing. I tried to eat as many snacks as possible, but I would go days without food sometimes, and it definitely showed in my weight loss. Now, for me, I could stand to lose some weight. When I noticed how the weight had begun to slip away, I used that weight loss to fuel a better way of eating and a healthier lifestyle overall.

We must constantly remind ourselves of all the ones still alive counting on us. If at first, you can't find the strength to keep going, find the strength in living for those who count on you. I had to find the strength to keep going in my children. I knew that if I fell apart (Lord knows I wanted to), there would be no one for my kids. Dad was gone, and he wasn't coming back. The kids were hurt and did not understand at all. They were looking to me for support and answers.

I had to be the strong one, whether I wanted to or not. This is where my faith was the most important. I gained my strength from God to be strong for them. It wasn't an option to give up, because if I did, I was not just giving up on me. I would be giving up on them, giving up on all the things waiting for me in the future.

Before it's over, the loneliness will begin to set in. This is when it's most important to surround yourself with people. This is the time to reach out to all those who said, "I'm here if you need to talk." I'm telling you this because it is very important that you surround yourself with positive people that know you. This is NOT the time to start any new friendships or relationships.

This is the time to trust in God and his word. Your emotions are raw, and your heart is broken. During this time, it is very easy to give time and energy to those who don't deserve it. It is even easier to fall into infatuation and mistake it for love. I am not saying that this will not be a future option, just not right now.

Always remember, our loved ones that pass on don't just decide to leave us. They still want all the best for us. They still want us to have love and companionship. They still want us to succeed in life. They still want all of our hopes and dreams to come true. They never intended for us to just stop living because they got a good ticket home. We must stop looking at death as this sorrowful time. We must look at death for what it really is, a celebration. People who die for whatever reason, maybe tragic or simply old age, are the chosen ones. They have been chosen to go be with our father, The King. We, the ones left behind, are who we should shed tears for. We are the ones stuck here, waiting to be chosen.

Remember Gods Plan

"For I know the plans I have for you" says the Lord, "plans
to prosper you and not to harm you, Plans to give you hope
and a future"

(Jeremiah 29:11).

So ......You want the key to understanding and dealing with death? Do you really? The real key to it all is trusting God and his plans for his children.

God told us from the beginning that he is our father. Like any other father, he is the master of our home. He makes all the decisions, and we are expected to do as we are told. If rules are broken or not appropriately followed, there will be consequences and repercussions. Our father can be strict, but his love is abounding. We, his children, can be easily bamboozled into thinking that we are in control of our lives. We are not.

God gives us the wiggle room to make decisions that will impact our lives in one way or another, sometimes for the positive, sometimes for the negative. The conundrum is God has a plan for us all. He had this plan before we were even planted into our mother's womb. We are all on this earth for a reason, unannounced to us.

A person will live their whole life just to be in a certain place at a certain time to speak to a particular person because that's what God needed from that person. Although it took a lot of years and a whole lot of pain, I was finally given a glimpse into the plan that God has for me.

On July 4, 2020, I was visiting with a childhood friend that had come back to our hometown of Detroit for a visit. Upon my arrival, I had the pleasure of meeting some family members of my girlfriend that I had not seen in so many years. One was a woman, a mother, with a sweet little girl sitting around not fazed in the slightest by all the colourful fireworks going off in the sky in every direction around her. We sat and talked and told stories of days past, and she told me of the life that I had missed. Later in the night, as we sat and talked, the mother began to tell her story.

Her story was filled with pain and hurt that sounded almost identical to a piece of mine. Her tears were so pure with emptiness and unanswered questions. A woman trapped in grief, struggling to find her way out all while being a mommy and working full time during the Covid-19 Quarantine.

As I sat and listened to her, I was filled with this need to stand. I mean, I could not sit still in the chair. Before I knew it, the words were spilling from my lips, the perfect scriptures to support my testimony. I know nothing, but God put his hands on me that night. I stood in testimony with so much passion that tears poured from my eyes, I stomped my feet and screamed into the darkness the praises of my God and his son. Now, I don't know how that night affected her, but I do know, I was given the opportunity by God to be there that night. I also knew I had been changed; something was in me that had to be released.

God led me to the people that could and would help me long ago; I just didn't know that at the time. I spoke to a spirit-filled woman that has been ordained by God to help people find their voice. She encouraged me to hear my calling and use all my pain to help others who have suffered like me by writing a book.

Some of us have higher callings to help, preach, heal, or teach. I believe this was God's plan for me all along. I could have never been the woman God needed me to be that night in July, had I not suffered all the loss that I have. I had a job to do, we all have a job to do as well, and when that mission is complete, God will bring us home for our reward to live in the peace and love of his arms. To be in a place where there is no pain or hurt.

We so easily take our relationships for granted. That could be our parents, children, or friends. We constantly think of them as ours; my mother, my father, my child, my friend. And again, we tend to lose track of what really is. Nope, they were Gods' first, and always will be. I used to think to myself, why did he have to take MY mother? He didn't; he brought HIS daughter home, as any good parent would do.

Anything and everything alive on this earth has a lifespan. From the moment we are born, we are on a track for death with a time clock hanging above our heads. Our time here is limited; this is why it is so important to stay on track and live by God's rules so that we may conquer our enemies, love our neighbours, do good deeds, and leave a positive mark on this world before we depart.

"For everything there is a season, and a time for every matter under heaven: a time to be born and a time to die; a time to plant, and a time to pluck what is planted" *(Ecclesiastes 3:1-2).*

Life is fragile and tumultuous while simultaneously being languorous but exciting. With all of this, we can take the word of God and use it as our shield against all the evils in the world as we go out on our paths, our footsteps guided by our father himself. It has been said in many ways, in song, in poetry, in literature, but in the end, it's all the same. This battle is not yours; it's the Lord's.

Finding the Strength to Take That First Step

"So do not fear, for I am with you; do not be dismayed, for I am your God. I will strengthen you and help you; I will uphold you with my righteous right hand"

(Isaiah 41:10).

At some point, after we have taken some time to heal, we will have to take the first step back to real life. This, for some of us, can be the hardest thing to do. Going back to work, or school, or life, in general, can be difficult. Facing all the people with those sad faces and all the condolences that were never given until they saw us again. The pressure to use our brain for something other than thinking of what we have lost. This is when we talk to God the most. This is when we need to ask for help.

Speaking to God is easy; we often think of him as this untouchable entity that we only call to in our hour of need, but that can't be farther from the truth. I was taught by a good friend that you should talk to God like you would speak to any other parent. Tell him your fears, goals, wants, dislikes, pains, worries, stresses, loves, anything that's on your mind at that time. We can also ask for things we need or want. Ask God for strength to carry on, understanding what you're feeling, relief from your mental and emotional pain, inner strength so that you may win the battle with your feelings.

Getting back to some type of normal is the ultimate goal. The question is what is normal now? That answer is anything you decide it to be. Life is what you make of it; whatever you were doing in the past may not be what you return to. Especially for me, every time I suffered a loss, I was changed. Each time I had to learn to live again with this new person I called me.

Figuring out how to live again without them was a test within itself. Something as simple as waking up in the morning was completely different without them; the worst was not having my man in the bed next to me. I couldn't figure out what to do with all the extra time I now had on my hands because I no longer had the person that I wanted to give all my time to. For me, I began to work out daily. It started with just my walks to clear my mind; by the end, I was pace walking 12 miles daily. With all the exercise, my free time was being used constructively.

Before I knew it, I had lost over 50 pounds, and I was a whole new woman. To go with my new life and my new body, I decided to get a new haircut, and I was transformed into a whole new person ready to face this whole new life God had given to me. Please understand that all this took place over some years, and still today, I am a work in progress every day. I think all is well, and one day I will catch a scent of cologne my husband wore on the wind, and it will take me back to tears and sadness.

The hardest is still and always will be the holidays. Sadly for me, even to this day, I have chosen not to celebrate most of them. I was talking to someone, and he asked, "So you're over all the loss now, right?" he continues, "I mean, if you're writing a book, you must be able to say you're over it." I was lost for an answer to the question because there was no true answer to it. Yes, I am over it as much as any person can be. I live my life; I am no longer struggling to just survive life. I am, for the most part, happy.

Life is still hard; each day, I think of those lost, and each day I still feel that pain of losing them. As time goes by, the pain becomes a mere pinprick, but I will never be completely numb to it. The process of writing this book has caused me to tap back into feelings that have been filed away into a deep recess of my heart so that I would never have to feel it again. The pain, for once, felt like a release.

So, here I am, five years have passed by already since my love took his leave. I have lost so much and so many people over the years. With each and every loss, I thought I would never make it through, never be able to cope. I learned new lessons; most of all, I learned just how strong I really am.

The most important lesson I learned is no matter what I am dealing with in my life; I am my strongest with God by my side. That I can't make it without God, and that no matter what I maybe feeling inside, I am never alone.

About the Author

Kenya Stevenson is a mother, an author and experienced chef with some 25 years of experience in busy kitchens. Above all, however, she is a survivor of multiple personal losses that have included the suicide of her mother and the sudden deaths of her infant son and husband.

Throughout it all Kenya has maintained her faith and ability to cope with the help and guidance she has received from God. It was with His direction and protection that she was able to emerge from her sorrow and find the strength and courage to help others do the same.

Now she has written a book, God, Why Me?, which details her struggles and explores grief and how to cope with it. It also provides the reader with mechanisms that will prevent grief from destroying your life and help you to find the peace you deserve.

Kenya's mission in life is to help those who find it hard to see beyond their grief, to show them that they are never alone in their fight and that it is a journey that cannot be avoided. Through the way she dealt with her own experiences, she is convinced that you too can heal and be happy once more.

Kenya's greatest achievements remain her children. She is dedicated to providing them with happy and fulfilling lives and works to ensure this each and every day.

You may reach Kenya via the following

https://www.facebook.com/kenya.stevenson.365

kenyastevenson365@gmail.com

kenyastevenson.com

"I am the vine, you are the branches, if you remain in me and I in you, you will bear much fruit; apart from me you can do nothing"

(John 15:15)

Made in the USA
Monee, IL
08 December 2020